Bitcoin

EXPRESS

Bitcoin Express

Bitcoin

EXPRESS

Know How Does Bitcoin Work and How
to Use It like Money

David Neal & KnowIt Express

N2K Publication

ISBN 978-1-533-05269-8

Printed in the United States of America

First Edition

Welcome to the *Know It Express* - the express lane to knowledge!

To stay up-to-date, please be sure to sign up for **our newsletter** at http://www.KnowItExpress.com and follow us on social media:

https://www.facebook.com/KnowItExpress
https://twitter.com/KnowItExpress
https://plus.google.com/+KnowItExpress

Bitcoin Express

EXPRESS LANE

CHAPTER 1 - Understanding the Revolutionary Monetary Technology Bitcoin

11 - The Future Of Money

14 - Bitcoin Explained

16 - Quiz: Making Bitcoin Work For You

CHAPTER 2 - Setting Everything Up with Bitcoin

19 - Obtain A Wallet

23 - Buy Bitcoin To Use

25 - The Value Of Bitcoin

CHAPTER 3 - Working with the Science and System of Bitcoin

27 - The Gold And Bitcoin Comparison

28 - Bitcoin Mining

32 - The Associated Risks And Rewards

CHAPTER 4 - Using and Incorporating Bitcoin in Everyday Life

36 - Put The Coin To Use

37 - Online Purchases

41 - In-Person Purchases

43 - For Payment Processing

43 - PayPal VS Bitcoin

44 - Credit Cards VS Bitcoin

45 - Digital Gift Cards VS Bitcoin

46 - Other Acceptable Processors

CHAPTER 5 - Making Money from Bitcoin?

48 - Navigating Uncharted Water

50 - Protecting Your Investments

CHAPTER 6 - Reviewing Bitcoin to Put It All Together

53 - Take The Next Step

56 - Proceed With Caution

58 - Know Bitcoins

59 - Know Mining

61 - *CHAPTER 7* - Closing Bitcoin to Get Started with Bitcoin

Bitcoin Express

CHAPTER 1

Understanding the Revolutionary Monetary Technology Bitcoin

The Future Of Money

So you are searching for some more *'cha-ching'* in your pockets?

Good, because that's what we're here to discuss! If you're looking for a cheap meal to cook for your lovely spouse, we're not talking to you right now.

<u>Challenge Number One</u>: gathering the money.

<u>Challenge Number Two</u>: keeping, growing, and using your money. But what's the best way to do so? How do you allocate it?

There are way too many options to count here.

- There are traditional options such as buying gold and silver, bank accounts, stock portfolios, and land or other property. Then there are forms of digital money, like PayPal, Amazon gift cards, and online credit cards...to touch just the tip of an immense iceberg.

But how do you sort through all the gimmicks and find an option that works for you right away?

Bitcoin! *No, this isn't an advertisement.* Continue on to find out <u>IF</u> bitcoin is right for you:

A.) What bitcoin is and generally how it works.

B.) How to make it work for you.

C.) Other good options and how they compare.

Each part will help you discover more about what this newest **internet sensation** is all about and how it works. As well as how to make money off of it, why to do so, and some warning signs to watch out for along the way.

Are you ready to dive into the world of bitcoin? Let's get started!

Bitcoin Explained

First of all, what the heck is bitcoin? You probably wouldn't be here without at least having heard of it, but let's start from the beginning.

Story time...

Once upon a time, the founders of the United States of America made it *illegal* to make your own money. Then one day, a man named **Bernard von NotHaus** disobeyed this law by making his own novel currency. It was called the Liberty Dollar. Uncle Sam caught and arrested him on charges of counterfeiting. But a hacker with the alias '**Satoshi Nakamoto**' emailed him saying that Bernard's Liberty Dollar inspired him to invent a new type of money altogether. He did. Satoshi invented his money system, put it out into the public internet...and *vanished*. To this day, no one knows who Satoshi Nakamoto is. *But thousands, maybe millions, of people are using his currency: bitcoin*.

But what is bitcoin, really?

Bitcoin isn't really money—it's a **code**.

Satoshi used mathematics to create the 'perfect' monetary system. A brand new **currency**. Bitcoin is the first widely used, 100% online currency with nothing physical to represent it.

- OK that's not entirely true: there are now places that you can **buy actual coins** that are *embedded with the value* of what you paid for them digitally, but the essence of bitcoin is online.

Bitcoin is, by its nature, extraordinarily secure. It has built-in securities that make it impossible to create or counterfeit. Because the code and all transactions are public, the code automatically keeps tabs on every last 'coin,' so it can't be stolen. And because of its public nature, no one entity can control it—ever. Not a person, not a business, not even a government.

We should clarify that although the transactions are public, which is key to bitcoin's operating and security, the identities of those making the transactions are not. The fact that <u>person X</u> gave <u>Y bitcoins</u> to <u>person Z</u> is public knowledge, as is the quantity $\underline{Y}$, but the identities of $\underline{X}$ and $\underline{Z}$ are *unknown*. This privacy is one of bitcoin's greatest attractions for many people.

<u>Quiz</u>: Making Bitcoin Work For You

So how can you use bitcoin and make it profitable for you? Is it worth it to get involved at all? How do you join if no one is in charge of it?

It wouldn't be surprising if you still have questions.

Let's take it *one step* at a time. First, let's find out if bitcoin is even useful for you with the following <u>quiz chart</u>. (The results will follow afterward.)

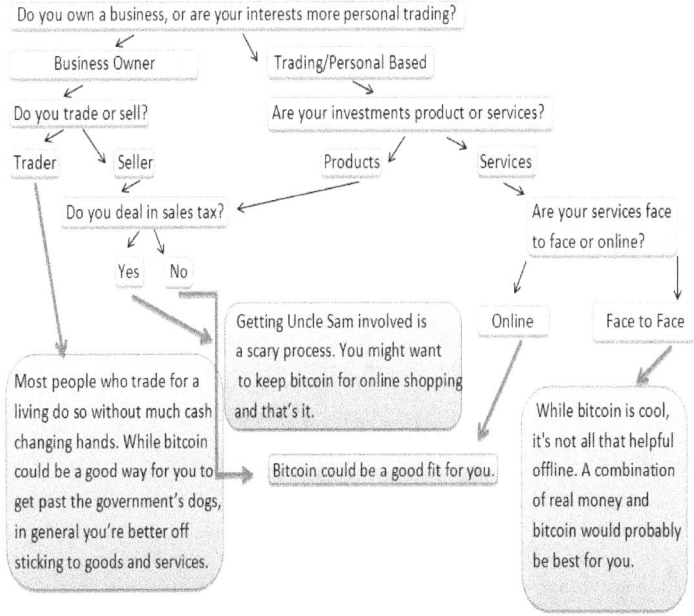

Understanding Your Results:

Answer #1:

Most people who trade for a living do so without much cash changing hands. While bitcoin could be a good way for you to get past the government's dogs, in general you're better off sticking to goods and services.

Feel free to keep going if you're curious, but bitcoin probably isn't the best for you.

Answer #2:

Getting Uncle Sam involved is a scary process. You might want to keep bitcoin for online shopping and that's it.

Again, proceed on if you're curious, but this probably won't help you much.

Answer #3:

Bitcoin could be a good fit for you.

Congratulations! Continue on fellow bitcoiner and we'll help you get started.

Answer #4:

While bit coin is cool, it's not all that helpful offline. A combination of real money and bitcoin would probably be the best for you.

What follows will be geared towards online work, but feel free to go to the end and see how it could apply to your business.

CHAPTER 2

Setting Everything Up with Bitcoin

Obtain A Wallet

So now, we're ready to put the pedal to the metal by first obtaining a **wallet.**

Yes, you heard that right. Bitcoins are online, but you need some way to *store your money* and *make your transactions.* There are several types of wallets, including ones for different devices.

<u>STEP ONE</u>: Pick your wallet. On https://bitcoin.org/en/choose-your-wallet you'll be introduced to bitcoin on the official website, where they can tell you almost anything about bitcoin for beginners. The part of their website you want to look at first is this page right here:

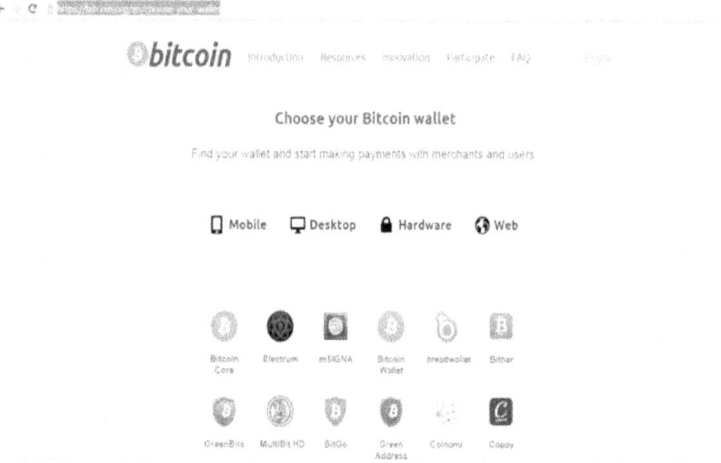

<u>STEP TWO</u>: Open up that **wallet**, and set it up on your phone *and/or* computer. These are the two places that you can put a bitcoin wallet, and you can use either one for transactions. The phone app uses **barcodes** so

you can simply touch your phone to the buyer/seller's and BAM! Your transaction is finished.

Once you've picked the wallet you want, click on it and hit 'install.' That should take you to a <u>page</u> similar to this one:

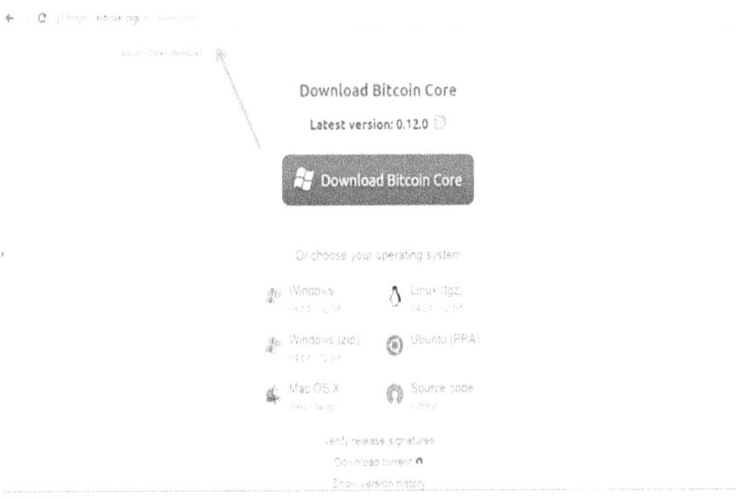

STEP THREE: Use it. *How?* Well in order to use the wallet you've now downloaded, you'll need to start buying, selling, and trading in the stuff—that means buying your very first bitcoin. For that, you need somewhere to trade, which we will get into next.

Buy Bitcoin To Use

After obtaining your wallet, the next part now involves buying bitcoins to use.

STEP ONE: Open up your **web browser** and type https://www.coinbase.com/signup. It should take you to a page that looks like this:

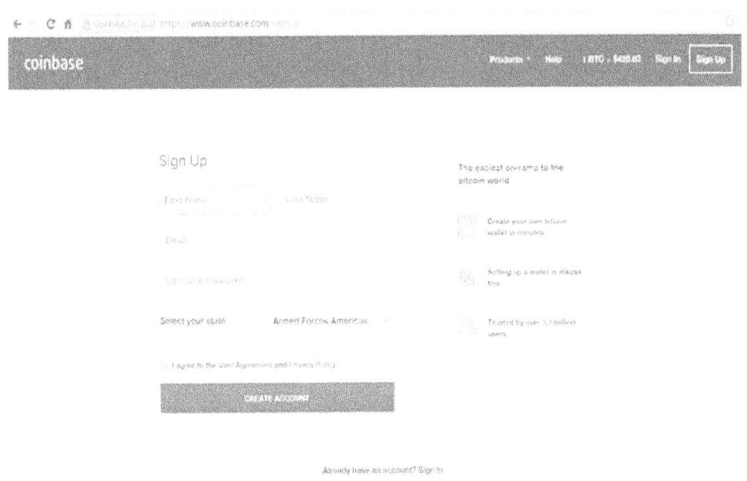

STEP TWO: Sign up and make your very **own account.** It will ask you to verify your **email,** so pick one that you use often, or one that you at least check and can remember the password to.

STEP THREE: Security is taken seriously on this account, so you'll need to provide other backup information (i.e., phone number, etc.) so that they have a way to make sure it's you. They will also use this information later on in the setup process.

STEP FOUR: Use your new bitcoin account! (Which looks like this.)

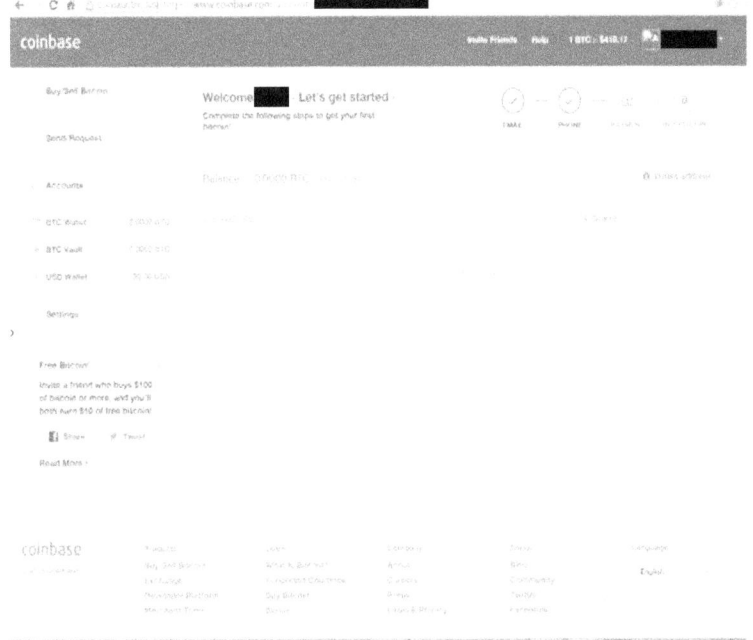

The Value Of Bitcoin

Now at this point, there is something about bitcoin that **you need to know.**

Bitcoins are worth a lot of money ($419.17 a coin currently). Don't fret!

Bitcoins are easily *broken down* into very small pieces so you can start out with buying or selling $10 worth of bitcoin, or less. But it will show up as 0.0025 or some similarly low number in your account.

There are also many other websites, besides Coinbase, that you can use to open an account for your bitcoin storage and use, but Coinbase is nice and easy.

CHAPTER 3

Working with the Science and System of Bitcoin

The Gold And Bitcoin Comparison

Now we're going to delve into the inner-workings of bitcoin.

Let's be honest, bitcoin can get rather technical. It's like trying to explain what the internet was in the early 90s. *But don't panic!* We'll be going over it in <u>baby steps</u>.

Think of bitcoin as digital gold:

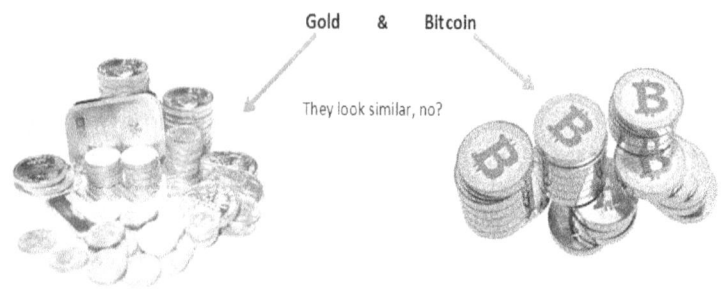

Gold & Bitcoin

They look similar, no?

Like gold, there is a limited number of bitcoin in the world (21 million, to be exact). But it's not all in circulation yet. It needs to be 'mined.'

Bitcoin Mining

So what is mining for bitcoin, how does it work, why would you do it, and are there securities in it?

Let's answer each question one at a time.

1.) What is mining for bitcoin?

In order for bitcoin to remain safe, the transactions between two people have to be verified, or confirmed, and then put down in the public ledger of all bitcoin transactions. (Remember how we said the code keeps tabs on all the coins and where they go over the entire world? That's the **ledger**.) Verifying the transactions can't be done by only one person, or else the entire system could be corrupted by that one person. So '**miners**' compete to do it first and are rewarded for their efforts with brand new bitcoin, 'mined' from the system.

2.) How does it work?

The code spits out a **math problem** that takes about ten minutes to solve. Think of the answer as the '**magic number**.' All the miners race to see who can find the 'magic number' first and solve the problem. The person who does gets to verify all the transactions that happened while they were solving it, about ten minutes worth of transactions all around the world. Then the next math problem is generated. Each problem is unique to one of the new bitcoins that is waiting to be 'mined.' So solving the problem 'mines' bitcoin unique to that problem, but it also lets you verify that other people's transactions happened fairly. This probably seems overly complicated—and if you don't understand it completely, don't worry—but this is intentional. The complexity of mining and verification is part of why bitcoin is so safe, as we'll explain.

3.) Why would you do it?

Most importantly to keep the system working, if the transactions went without verification there would be nothing at all to keep the transactions smooth and safe. Anyone could take bitcoin from anyone for anything. It wouldn't be money; it'd be chaos. So the more miners are out there mining for new bitcoin, the safer the system is because there are hundreds of people who are watching everyone else. Plus you are paid to do it with new bitcoin to spend (if you succeed).

4.) Are there securities in it?

This depends on what kind of security you mean. Security in the system—yes. Security for you as the miner—no. In order to keep the math problem long enough that it takes ten minutes to solve, the problems have to change according to how many people are looking for it. So with lots of people looking, the problems tend to look like this:

*****

With so much math to solve for only ten minutes of verification, and hundreds of thousands of people looking, you need special computers and equipment to find the 'magic number.' That means investing in the machinery and the time.

Does this make it a good investment? Maybe. But just like prospectors of old who dug up gold with pickaxes, you might also work yourself to the bone and never hit pay dirt.

The Associated Risks And Rewards

Obviously if you're using money in any form, there is always **risk** involved.

- Carrying an actual wallet, you can be pickpocketed; shopping online, someone can steal your credit card information, etc.

Bitcoin is no different. So let's go over what makes bitcoin sensible and not so sensible. Starting with the <u>key</u> below:

Why you WANT Bitcoin	Why you RATHER NOT use Bitcoin
*No Government Control	*More Flux
*Security of Self	*No Backups or Safe Houses
*Genuine Increase in Value	*Pull of Illegal Activity

Using the key above, let's look at some of the risks, and securities in more depth, with a brief overview and specific examples of each.

<u>Row #1</u> – No Government Control & More Flux:

Because of bitcoin's nature as an open currency, there is nothing and no one to control or dictate it. This can be a good thing because you are completely free to mine, trade, sell, or buy 'coins' without anyone looking over your shoulder. But this can also be damaging because it isn't likely to make everyone rich, only a few. This means that, because you're still new to it, you may be the one to get the short end of the stick. And, of course, the value in "the real world" jumps up and down like a yo-yo, making it impossible to predict.

Row #2 – Security of Self & No Backups or Safe Houses:

Because bitcoin is a digital online currency, there is the possibility of others stealing it from you as you use it, or from the source that you use online in your account to 'bank' it. This means that you are more responsible for your own money. While this can be a good thing for your personal peace of mind, it can also make it too easy for the criminal element. There are, of course, securities in the bitcoins themselves, and most accounts or servers (like Coinbase) take all kinds of measures to keep your money safe. But hacking is an unfortunate reality that must be considered in anything digital.

Row #3 – Genuine Increase in Value & Pull of Illegal activity:

As mentioned above, criminals use bitcoin because it is so hard to monitor. You may have heard about the closure of 'Silk Road,' a black market website. However, it was widely used for its honest and genuine value as well as by criminals. Now, the value of bitcoin can easily increase or decrease. It's something that will become more stable, as well as more valuable, the more people that are involved use it. So the faster and more you use it, the better it will become with time, you just have to know how to stick with it.

CHAPTER 4

Using and Incorporating Bitcoin in Everyday Life

Put The Coin To Use

So you now have a bitcoin account, but how do you actually use it? Especially if it can be risky to do so?

To answer these questions and to help you out, we start things off with two real life examples below to illustrate bitcoin utilization.

Online Purchases

Since many places in the U.S. do not like to accept bitcoin <u>DIRECTLY</u>, there are a couple of options.

- You might send the bitcoin through a bank, and then spend the money in your account. But that takes days to verify—then why use bitcoin at all?

- You can instantly transfer bitcoin with <u>gyft</u>. **Gyft** is both a *website* and an *app* that will let you buy **gift cards** to just about anywhere, and they accept bitcoin!

<u>Here's how</u>:

1.) First, open an account with <u>gyft.com</u> on the main website. Then it will take you to your account (see the screenshot below).

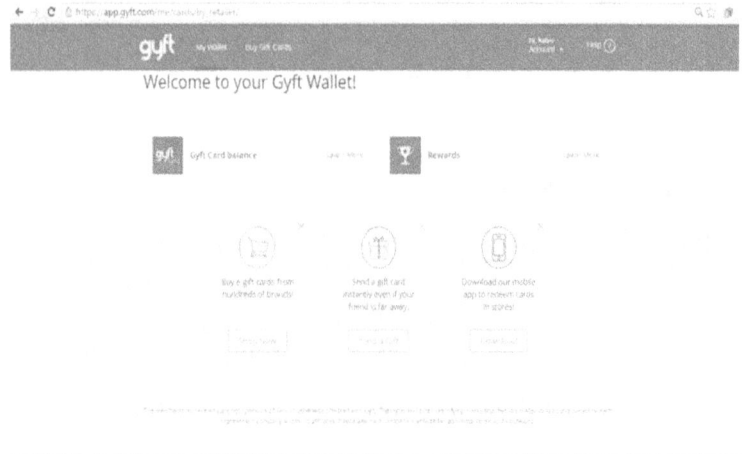

2.) Second, click on the <u>orange box</u> with the **shopping cart icon**. It will take you to a page that will let you shop for gift cards.

3.) Third, once you've selected a card, it will give you the option to *buy for yourself* or *send to someone else.* Click on **buy for yourself** (for now). It'll take you to this page.

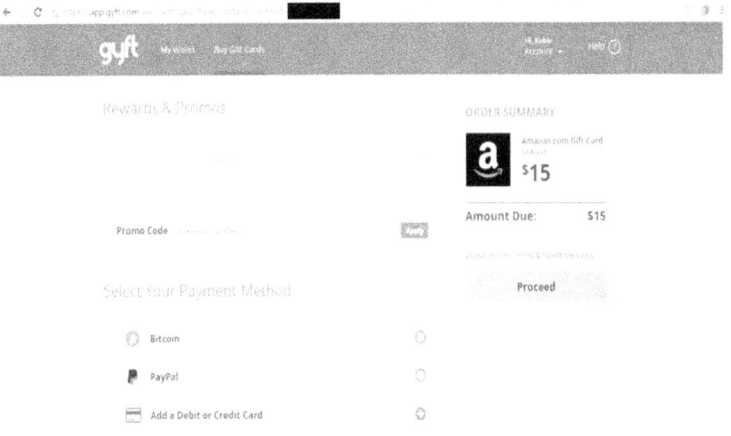

4.) Select "**Bitcoin**" as your payment method, and then select "**Proceed.**"

5.) It will take you to a page that asks you to choose between <u>two bitcoin sources</u>. The account we showed you how to make earlier is with **Coinbase.** Once you've selected that, it will ask you to sign into your Coinbase account. Then it will take you to this page:

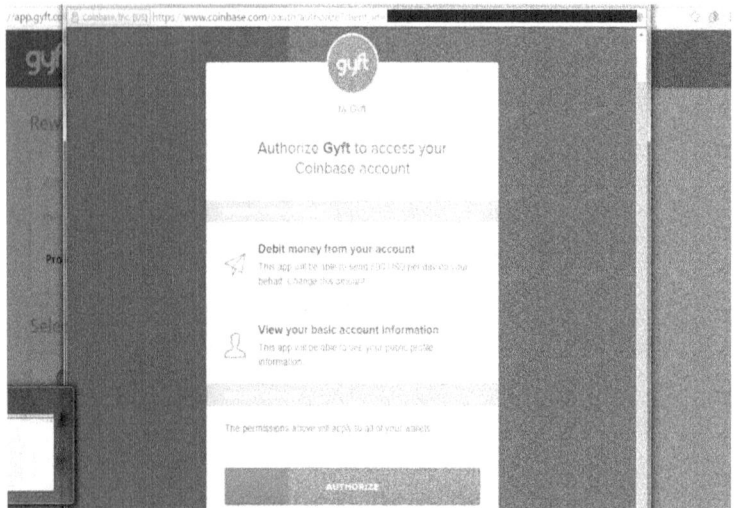

6.) Hit "**Authorize**," and it will link your **bitcoin account** to **gyft**. The purchase of your gift card will go through, and then you can use it to buy anything you'd like.

In-Person Purchases

In some places in the U.S. and many more in Europe, there are shops that actually accept bitcoin as payable money.

All you need is an internet connection on your phone. You can get onto your account at any time to find a **barcode** for your transaction. The barcodes look something like this:

This barcode can be scanned by **phone** or **tablet**, photographed, or sent by putting two phones or tablets side-by-side. This will automatically send your bitcoin to their store.

- Just make sure that you have a "**QR code scanner**" app installed; if you don't, you can download one for free (by searching for it on the internet using your device, or from any app store, depending on which operating system you're on).

You can tell if a store will take bitcoin if it has <u>this sign</u> in the **window** or **front door**.

For Payment Processing

You may have come to believe that bitcoin is still too spanking new. *DON'T!*

While security has to be taken into account, and it can be complicated to understand technically, it's great for uses such as **payment processing**.

Let's take a look at three more common **online money options** that you probably use regularly and compare their pros and cons with bitcoin.

PayPal VS Bitcoin

PayPal	Bitcoin
Good: *Tons of extra security, you help control *Verified accounts of all transactions *User friendly	**Good**: *100% in charge of your own security *Faster/even more user friendly than PayPal *Completely free of fees and charges
Bad: *Some fees and charges on occasion *Can be slow to process *Have to trust PayPal to keep you safe	**Bad**: *100% in charge of your own security *Have to trust strangers for verifications *No backups or extra security

While PayPal is secure beyond belief, Bitcoin is something that you have to control the safety of yourself; and while this might make some people nervous, it is also easier to use.

- PayPal need days to process and can reject a transaction for any reason.

- Bitcoin is instant and will never be denied or rejected.

Credit Cards VS Bitcoin

Credit Cards	Bitcoin
Good: *Simple to understand and use online	**Good**: *Faster/simpler to use than cards
*Banks back them up with security	*Will never be frozen for any reason
*Automatic payments take away your cares	*No fees or charges – ever
Bad: *Many charges and fees for various uses	**Bad**: *No backups or bank security
*Can get stolen fairly easily	*Can get stolen fairly easily
*Can be shut down by the bank at any time	*Not able to be automated like cards

Again, the security seems like an issue, but with bitcoin, no hacker can get your identification.

Credit and debit cards lead to banks, and banks keep phone numbers, ID numbers, names, dates, and addresses. But if you lose bitcoin, all you lose is your money, not your identity.

Also all those pesky fees, payments, and charges are also gone! However, there are no cash back options either.

Digital Gift Cards VS Bitcoin

Digital Gift Cards	Bitcoin
Good: *Aren't linked to your bank account *Can buy anything you want *Don't clutter up your real wallet	Good: *Can buy whatever you want *Have no time limit or expiration date *Only spending limit is what you set
Bad: *Have a set amount you can use *Might need to be used within a certain timeframe *Limited to compatible sites	Bad: *They aren't 'gifts' *Used only on sites that are compatible *Have no way to return to you if lost

Everyone loves gift cards because it's literally someone else giving you money.

Well in that sense, bitcoin can't really compete. However, unlike gift cards that have expiration dates and specifications on where you can use them, bitcoin can be used anywhere for anything.

Just talk your sister into loaning you a few bucks to convert to bitcoin for that baby shower instead of a card to ToysRUs.

Other Acceptable Processors

There are several other options for online transactions, including WePay and Google Wallet. However, the three above are the ones that you are most likely to see and are representative of the alternatives.

If you're still unsure if bitcoin is for you, use the comparison charts above to check it against the other sources that you might already use.

Now that you've seen the comparisons and how you can get it to work in your favor, what will you do with the information?

CHAPTER 5

Making Money from Bitcoin?

Navigating Uncharted Water

Of course, this is the part that everybody looks forward to: how to make a fast buck without much effort!

Well sorry to break it to you, but with territory this new, you'll still have to be putting in the effort if you want to take advantage of the bitcoin phenomenon. That's just the way it works.

Nevertheless, here are a few things that will help you out.

- **Understand the difference between a 'wallet' and a 'vault.'** Wallets are designed to be easy to use, but are likewise easy to lose. The same logic applies to bitcoin—don't take your whole life savings out with you, leave some of it at home. (There is a vault option in Coinbase.com.)

- **Know your fees.** Bitcoin is basically free, but some places (like Coinbase) will ask for 1% or less to return bitcoin to the form of actual money, because many banks do not recognize them.

- **Be aware of scams.** All bitcoin transaction are 100% buyer beware. If you lose the money that you put in, you're not likely to get it back. So be cautious in all your dealings, but don't lose faith in the system altogether. There are a lot of legit companies and people out there too.

- **In the case of a stolen wallet, act FAST.** Unlike stealing a real wallet, hackers don't have actual access to the coins inside until they are moved, or 'spent.' So they will 'spend' them by moving them to their own wallets. Of course, this is something that happens rather quickly, but it is possible to save your coins by spending them yourself before the hacker can. Either by buying something large, or moving them all to a separate wallet with another password. It's not much of a trick, but it's far better than being unable to do anything at all about it.

- **Keep it clean.** Cybercriminals work to break into wallets and vaults, but keeping your malware definitions up to date and your PC clear can cut them out.

Protecting Your Investments

Here are other steps to take:

- Encrypting your wallets will make them harder to hack.

- Use various wallets for different purposes.

- Don't store large amounts or put your life savings into bitcoin all at once.

- Keep bitcoin off your mobile unless in VERY small amounts, as mobile devises are easier to crack or loose.

You've likely noticed that almost all of these tips and tricks have something to do with security.

There is a very good reason for this. Because bitcoin is an open market, there is no one way to make a lot of money off it at once, or at all.

There is no 'best' way to get the money to work for you, and you can't tell anyone how to correctly invest in it. This means that how you use bitcoin is completely up to you. All we can tell you is the best way to keep it safe while you do so.

Your best bet, however, would be to approach buying bitcoins as you would investing in stocks, with the hope that their value will go up. It's uncharted and risky, but it can also be rewarding to be one of the pioneers. It certainly worked out for Kristoffer Koch whose $27 (yes, plain double digits twenty-seven dollars) worth of "forgotten bitcoins" is now worth close to a million dollars.

All great investors have one thing in common: great foresight. Keep yourself up-to-date with the ever-changing nature of bitcoin, because you could...*lose it all* or *win it all*.

Is that a risk you're willing to take?

CHAPTER 6

Reviewing Bitcoin to Put It All Together

Take The Next Step

Now let's go back over the basics briefly, in case you want to start now:

1.) You use bitcoin with an account called a **wallet**, where you can *store and keep tabs* on your bitcoin, along with a **secondary account** where you can *trade and sell*.

Pick your first wallet and download it.

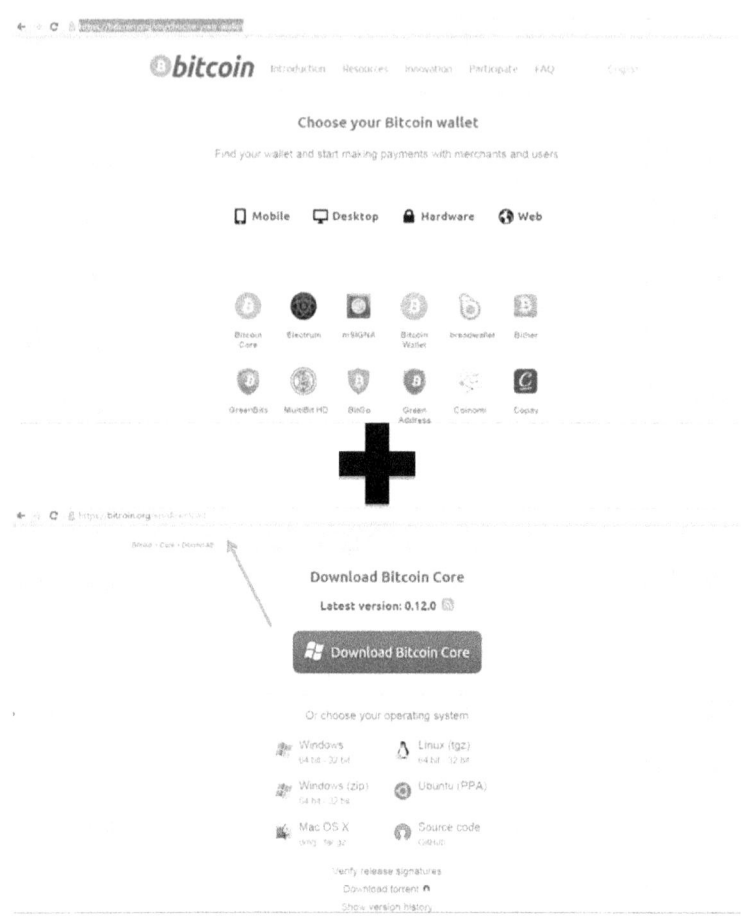

2.) Sign up on a platform to trade and sell on it.

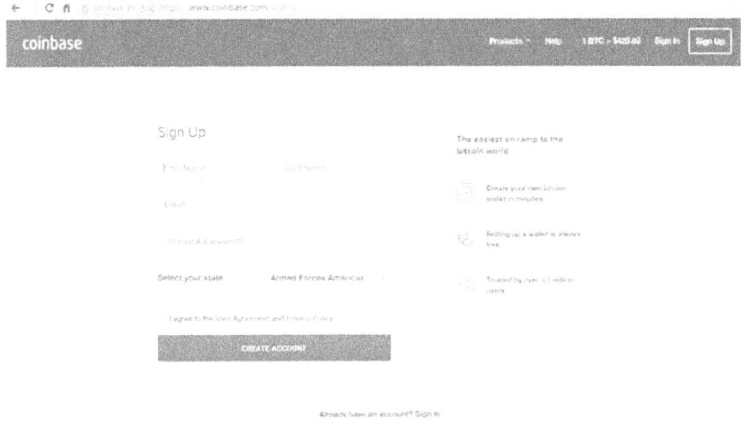

3.) Use these bitcoins both online and off.

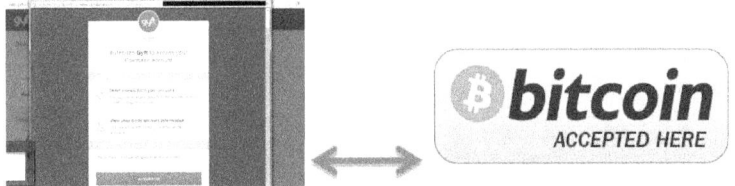

Didn't take more than a minute, did it?

Proceed With Caution

You should take security measures to safeguard your bitcoins, and remember the risks involved:

- Understand the difference between a 'wallet' and a 'vault.'

- Know your fees.

- Be aware of scams.

- In the case of a stolen wallet—act FAST.

- Keep it clean.

- Encrypt your wallets.

- Use more than one wallet.

- Don't store in large amounts, or put life savings into bitcoin all at once.

- Keep bitcoin off your mobile.

Why you WANT Bitcoin	Why you RATHER NOT use Bitcoin
*No Government Control	*More Flux
*Security of Self	*No Backups or Safe Houses
*Genuine Increase in Value	*Pull of Illegal Activity

Know Bitcoins

But all of this means nothing if you don't know *what bitcoin is.*

It's a **digital money system** (or cryptocurrency) that is similar to gold in its workings online. (It's scarce, can be mined, can be stolen without a trace, etc.)

So now you've got a good grip on what bitcoin is, how it can be used by you, and how the alternatives compare.

You're ready to make an informed decision about how, if at all, you want to incorporate bitcoin into your life.

If you start now, you'll have the edge, being an early adopter, and perhaps even be able to help other friends and relatives get into this monetary technology.

Know Mining

Let's take another look at bitcoin mining, too:

When you 'mine' bitcoin, you're *adding* to the entire bitcoin economy, both by making more currency and by verifying transactions. However nearly everyone who gets involved in new currency without looking at *what it takes* looses everything.

Recall that the math gets harder and harder to do...

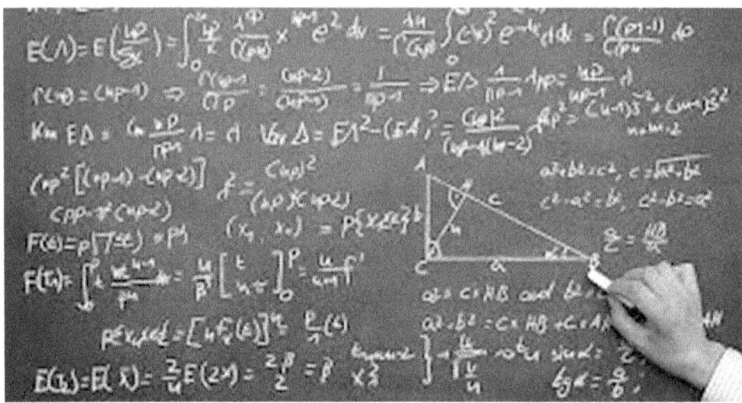

The special machines and computers that crunch these numbers cost money, and while you might be making more money by mining, if you don't do your homework, you're far more likely to end up with a waste of time, money, and electricity.

(Besides telling you all of this to save you **time,** we tell you all of this to save you **money**...and to save the planet from excess pollution due to wasted electricity).

CHAPTER 7

Closing Bitcoin to Get Started with Bitcoin

You now know what bitcoin is and where it came from, whether or not it will work for you, and how to start using it. You even know the beginnings of how to 'make' more of it by mining, as well as how it stacks up to traditional forms of online money.

So...now what? At the beginning, we asked a question.

- But how do you sort through all the gimmicks, and find an option that works for you right away?

If you've learned anything about bitcoin so far, you should have learned that it's something that you can start getting into now. There were even step-by-step instructions for how to open all your accounts so that you know what you are doing.

So now...go experiment with bitcoin!

In using it, be sure to remember the risks involved. If you use it in ways that minimize those risks, your chances of success will increase substantially.

Who knows, bitcoin just might change your entire world, or at least the way you shop or do business—just as the internet has for all of us.

Bitcoin Express

Bitcoin Express

Now You Know!

We have now gone from - *NOT knowing*...to *KNOWING.*

Doesn't it feel great? As cliché as the proverbial saying goes: knowledge is, indeed, power. The more you know, the more empowered you become. Not knowing is defeating, as you succumb to feelings of helplessness and surrendering of your own self.

Of course, acquiring knowledge is a never-ending quest. There is a great saying by Nobel Prize French author Andre Gide: "Believe those who are seeking the truth. Doubt those who find it."

At the very least, we hope we have set you off in the right path in regards to what you have set out to know, and that you have enjoyed our little journey together for the time you have spent with us.

If you can tell us how we did, that would be very appreciated! We value your feedback and always look forward to hearing from you, or if there is any way we could improve the entire experience for you. If you have a success story, even better - please let us know!

http://www.KnowItExpress.com

Don't forget to stay in contact for we would love to connect with you.

https://www.facebook.com/KnowItExpress
https://twitter.com/KnowItExpress
https://plus.google.com/+KnowItExpress

What would you like to know? Let us know!

CONTACT US

Now onward for more power to you, and thank you!

Bitcoin Express